MAITREYA BODHISATTVA'S INQUIRY SUTRA

MAITREYA BODHISATTVA'S INQUIRY SUTRA

THE COMING BUDDHA

The Revelation of the Extraordinary Ways
of Bodhi Path Cultivation for Bodhisattvas

This sutra was translated from Pali into Chinese by
Bodhiruci (693-713 C.E.) and into English by

TZE-SI HUANG

Illustrated by

DEMI

FONS VITAE

First published in 2016 by
Fons Vitae
49 Mockingbird Valley Drive
Louisville, KY 40207
http://www.fonsvitae.com
Email: fonsvitaeky@aol.com

ISBN 978-1891785-313

Dedicated to Anam Thubten Rinpoche, Elizabeth Mattis Namgyel,
and Owsley Brown III, travellers on the Bodhisattva path.

Many thanks to Anne Ogden for tireless profreading.

Printed in Canada

Contents

Contents, continued

I DEER PARK

SIXTY SINFUL BODHISATTVAS

Thus have I heard. At that time the Buddha was staying in the Deer Park, in the company of a gathering of one thousand great Bhiksus (monks) and five hundred Bodhisattvas (those who aspire to the attainment of Buddhahood). Among these five hundred Bodhisattvas, there were sixty who had committed great sins and misdeeds in the past. They were dull and foolish: they indulged in worldly speech and pleasures; they slept too much and were sluggish; they loved senseless chatter; engaged in various worldly business; succumbed to varieties of greed and did wrong things; they digressed from right thoughts; practiced "wrong wisdom" and were cunning; and they were confused and lax in the right cultivation of the Dharma (the teaching given by the Buddha).

MAITREYA BODHISATTVA

The great Maitreya Bodhisattva, seeing these Bodhisattvas falling from the right path, thought to himself that he could help dispel their confusion and direct them to the right path.

Then Maitreya Bodhisattva appeared in their abode to comfort them with gentle words and expounded the essence of the right Dharma to cheer them up. Maitreya Bodhisattva asked, "How do you cultivate and advance yourselves on the Bodhi (enlightenment) path?" The Bodhisattvas answered simultaneously, "We are no longer able to make any progress on the Bodhi path, instead we are regressing. Because our hearts and minds are clouded with doubts, we cannot understand the Supreme Bodhi Path anymore. We also waver as to whether we should continue to proceed on the Path or not; we are not sure about the

law of Karma (actions and deeds); we are not certain whether we are falling from the Path. Hence we do not know how to move forward."

BUDDHA'S ADMONITIONS

Maitreya Bodhisattva suggested that they seek guidance from the Buddha, the All-Knower, who could guide them in the right direction. They, then, all went with Maitreya Bodhisattva to the abode of the Buddha. They prostrated themselves and touched the Buddha's feet with their heads. They were so overcome by their sorrows that they wept and could not get up. Buddha told them to get up and not to cry anymore. Then Buddha said, "In the past, you derived great pleasure by cursing, insulting and slandering people, practicing discrimination according to your own biases, ignoring your own misconducts and the consequences; hence, you are now enshrouded with negative karmas and as such you are not able to follow the right way to make progress on the Bodhi Path.

Having heard the Buddha, they rose from their seats in the assembly, uncovered their right shoulders, placed their right knees on the ground, put their hands together with respect and said, "World Honored One, marvelous, marvelous! Thank you for telling us the sins and misdeeds we have committed. Now we all know our past sins and wish to rectify them. Starting from today, we will not dare to repeat those sins again."

The Buddha continued, "In the time of ancient Buddhas, you joined the order to seek enlightenment. Because you were so proud of your knowledge and practice of the precepts, you became arrogant and overbearing. At that time, there were two Bhiksus (monks) who expounded the Dharmas and were highly respected by their followers. Due to jealousy you slandered them by spreading rumors that they committed improper sexual acts. As a result, their followers left them. Hence you cut off the good roots for those followers. For this sin, you fell into the four hells for a total period of eighteen million years. After that you were born into the human world. For five hundred lives you were born blind and disabled, defective, retarded, stupid, ugly, poor and looked down upon by other people.

Then in the first five hundred years of the Dharma declining period, you were born into debased families in remote and desolate places, and suffered starvation. You were slandered, abused and had numerous difficulties. Finally your sins were eliminated. You will be born into The Pure Land of Amida; in the future you will eventually reach Buddhahood."

THIRTEEN GREAT VOWS

Hearing these words, the Bodhisattvas were deeply distressed. They said, "World Honored One, we deeply repent our sins and solemnly make the following major vows:

From today to the infinite future, if we expose the faults of other Bodhisattvas, we will be cheating Tathagata.

From today to the infinite future, if we ridicule, insult, become jealous or detest other Bodhisattvas, we will be cheating Tathagata.

From today to the infinite future, if we see other Bodhisattvas participating in and enjoying the five worldly desires, we will not look at their faults. Instead we will continue to respect them and consider them as our teachers. If not, we will be cheating Tathagata.

From today to the infinite future, for those Bodhisattvas who are respected and offered benefits by their followers, we will not be jealous or do anything to cause them distress. If not, we will be cheating Tathagata.

From today to the infinite future, if we use rude, coarse or vulgar language about other Bodhisattvas, we will be cheating Tathagata.

From today to the infinite future, if we do not maintain proper courtesy and respect for other Bodhisattvas at all times, without fail, we will be cheating Tathagata.

From today to the infinite future, we will uphold our vows even at the risk of our own lives. If not, we will be cheating Tathagata.

From today to the infinite future, if we do not respect other Sravakas and Pratekyabuddas, and even consider them less, we will be cheating Tathagata.

From today to the infinite future, if we cannot overcome our defects, be humble and self-effacing, we will be cheating Tathagata.

From today to the infinite future, if we engage in self-praise and put down others, we will be cheating Tathagata.

From today to the infinite future, if we do not stay away, as far as possible, from places of conflict and dispute, we will be cheating Tathagata.

From today to the infinite future, if we show off our efforts in the practice of precepts, desirelessness, and learning as well as all merits and virtues, we will be cheating Tathagata.

From today to the infinite future, if we are proud of our own accomplishments but don't reveal our faults and repent, we will be cheating Tathagata.

At that time, Buddha commended the Bodhisattvas and said, "Very good, very good. Good men, very well said to make such extensive vows. With determination to uphold these vows, all your sins will be eliminated, and unlimited good roots will grow."

II MAITREYA BODHISATTVA'S INQUIRY

Then Buddha told Maitreya Bodhisattva, "Maitreya, if Bodhisattvas wish to remove their sins, they should make and uphold such extensive vows." Maitreya Bodhisattva asked Buddha, "World Honored One, can good men and good women who uphold these extensive vows reach enlightenment without regression?" Buddha told Maitreya Bodhisattva, "If good men and good women on the Bodhi Path can uphold these extensive vows even at the risk of their own lives, they will not regress." Maitreya Bodhisattva continued, "World Honored One, for Bodhisattvas in the first five hundred years of the declining period of Buddhism, what Dharmas must they accomplish in order to achieve the state of peace without worries and reach ultimate liberation?"

Buddha told Maitreya Bodhisattva, "Maitreya, in the first five hundred years of the declining period of Buddhism, Bodhisattvas should accomplish four Dharmas to achieve the state of peace without worries and reach ultimate liberation.

FOUR DHARMAS FOR LIBERATION

"What are the four Dharmas?

> "First do not see other people's faults.
>
> "Second, when Bodhisattvas commit misdeeds, do not expose them.
>
> "Third, do not attach (become jealous) or obstruct when family members or friends offer benefits to other Bodhisattvas.
>
> "Forth, do not engage in any kind of bad speech."

"Maitreya, in the first five hundred years of the declining period of Buddhism, Bodhisattvas who accomplish these four Dharmas will attain liberation." Then The World Honored One restated the gist of these Dharmas with these verses:

"Do not look for other's faults.

"Do not expose other's faults.

"Do not use vulgar, rude and violent language.

"One will attain liberation."

Buddha continued, "Maitreya, in the first five hundred years of the declining period of Buddhism, Bodhisattvas who accomplish four more Dharmas will achieve peace without worries and attain liberation.

FOUR MORE DHARMAS FOR LIBERATION

"What are the four more Dharmas?

"First, staying away from people who are lazy; (even though they may be very busy doing things which have nothing to do with Dharma cultivation).

"Second, staying away from noisy market places and people who indulge in clamorous activities.

"Third, staying in a quiet place and practicing Dharma with a straight mind, and being contented.

"Forth, utilizing various skillful ways to regulate oneself."

Then the World Honored One restated the gist of these Dharmas with the following verses:

"Give up indolence.

"Stay away from noisy market places and clamorous activities.

"Live in quietude and be contented.

"One will attain liberation."

Then the World Honored One told Maitreya Bodhisattva, "Maitreya, therefore in the first five hundred years of the declining period of Buddhism, Bodhisattvas who wish to live in peace without worries and to eliminate all their sins and obstacles in order to attain liberation should conduct themselves in the following way:

"Stay away from noisy market places and clamorous activities.

"Live in a quiet place.

"Stay away from people clouded with three poisons as well as those who are lazy and indolent.

"Find one's own faults and correct them and do not see other's faults.

"Dwell in quietude with joy and act with wisdom."

SPREADING THE DHARMAS

"Furthermore, if Bodhisattvas wish to spread the Dharma, it should be done with compassion and a pure heart to help others, and without thinking of receiving rewards."

Twenty Benefits

"Maitreya, Bodhisattvas who spread the Dharma by helping people with compassion and pure hearts, who are detached from fame, wealth and rewards, and without any thought of helping others, will gain the following twenty benefits:

"A pure heart and mind.

“An increase in insight.

“Fortitude.

“A virtuous and pure life.

“A growth in awareness.

“A gain in non-worldly wisdom.

“They will not be harmed by devils.

“A state of no greed.

“A state of no anger.

“A state of no ignorance.

“Blessings from Buddhas.

“Protection from spirits.

“Protection from heavenly beings.

“Benefits for family members.

“They will be articulate and believed by people.

“They will not be obstructed by enemies.

“They will be fearless.

“They will be joyous.

“They will be praised by wise people.

“They will be skilled in spreading the Dharma and admired and respected by people.

"Maitreya, these are the twenty benefits for Bodhisattvas who spread the Dharma to help others without hoping for fame, wealth or rewards."

Buddha continued, "Maitreya, in addition, Bodhisattvas who spread the Dharma to help people with compassion, pure hearts and minds, who are detached from fame, wealth and rewards, and are without the thought of helping others will gain another twenty benefits:

Twenty More Benefits

"They will achieve eloquence.

"They will never lose their eloquence.

"They will be able to grasp the essence of the Dharmas through cultivating diligently.

"They will be able to help unlimited numbers of people with skillful means and minimum effort.

"They will be able to inspire people with skillful means to appreciate and admire The Three Treasures:The Buddha, The Dharma and The Sangha.

"They will achieve purity of body, speech and mind.

"They will transcend all negative Karmas.

"They will remain joyous when they leave the world at the time of death.

"They will be able to defeat all heresies by expounding the right Dharma.

"They will reach the state beyond the state of rich and famous people as well as the poor.

"They will accomplish all good roots.

"They will attain great wisdom and ability without obstruction.

"They will achieve inner peace and happiness.

"They will attain inner stability of insight and Samadhi.

"They will attain Samatha (calmness of mind).

"They will be able to cultivate and accomplish the most complex Dharmas.

"They will have total devotion to the cultivation of Dharma.

"They will be able to protect the right Dharma.

"They will quickly attain to the state of non-regression.

"They will achieve total freedom from delusion and dwell in the natural state."

Buddha emphasized, "These are the twenty benefits Bodhisattvas will gain if they spread the Dharma with a pure heart and remain detached from fame, wealth and rewards."

VARIOUS PROBLEMS OF THE DHARMA DECLINING PERIOD

Greed for Offerings, and the like

Buddha told Maitreya Bodhisattva, "Maitreya, in the first five hundred years of the declining period of Buddhism, there will be many Bodhisattvas who do not have wisdom. They will be happy to spread the Dharma only when they are offered benefits and receive admiration from their followers. In addition, in order to seek benefits, they will grab followers and keep them for themselves. These misguided Bodhisattvas think that people should believe and respect them and provide them with offerings, clothes, foods, medicine, etc. They only promote the Dharma in exchange for wealth and benefits. If they do not get what they want, they think that it is senseless for them to promote the Dharma. They will then leave their followers."

Fifteen Deviant Things

There are fifteen things Buddha would not say.

Buddha said, "Maitreya,

"I would not say that individuals who spread the Dharma with the desire for benefits are pure. Why? Because a greedy mind cannot see equality.

"I would not say that those whose minds are clouded with the three poisons are able to help others to attain liberation. Why? Since they have not attained liberation themselves it is impossible for them to help others attain liberation.

"Maitreya,

"I would not say that individuals who are looking for pleasure, respect and offerings with inappropriate means are able to help others. Why? Since they are only interested in having a good life for themselves. It is not possible for them to inspire others to develop and maintain real faith.

"Maitreya,

"I would not say that individuals who pretend to stay in simple, quiet places, practice desirelessness and to be contented as a means to gain fame and benefits are pure.

"Maitreya,

"I would not say that those who are actively looking for exquisite, high-quality clothes are compatible to the simple life of cultivators.

"Maitreya,

"I would not say that individuals, who have left home or not, trying to acquire fame can claim that they have stayed away from involvement in worldly marketplace activities.

"Maitreya,

"Also, I would not say that:

> "Individuals with a dishonest and crooked mind can meet a Buddha.
>
> "Individuals are cultivating the Dharma in the right way, if they still look at other people's faults.
>
> "Individuals are upholding the precepts if their minds still harbor the desire to hurt others.
>
> "Arrogant individuals are really knowledgeable.

"Maitreya,

"I would not say that:

> "Individuals who like to form cliques in an organization are able to abide by the rules.
>
> "Profane speech is the right expression of the Dharma.
>
> "Those who are arrogant can claim to respect their teachers or masters.
>
> "Monks and nuns who like to associate with worldly people won't make mistakes.

"Maitreya,

"I would not say that:

> "Individuals who donate with an arrogant mind are not seeking a reward.
>
> "Individuals who do good deeds with the purpose of self enrichment are pure.
>
> "Individuals who look for respect and offerings are pure.
>
> "Calculating and manipulating is the right behavior for monks and nuns.

"Maitreya,

"I would not say that:

"Individuals who discriminate are practicing the precepts.

"Individuals who listen to the Dharma exposition without respect are listening in the right way.

"Those cultivators who are interested in worldly books, speech and exorcisms have obtained the right Dharma.

"Maitreya,

"I would not say that:

"Individuals without full understanding of the nature of 'emptiness' can get out of the birth and death cycle.

"Individuals who still cling to worldly matters can claim that they have put everything down.

"Maitreya,

"I would not say that:

"Individuals who claim that they have attained liberation have really attained anything.

"Maitreya,

"I would not say that:

"Those who lack the ability or courage to respond to insults can claim they have accomplished the virtue of enduring insults.

"Those who claim they have accomplished the strength of stability, without experiencing any temptations, have accomplished the attribute of stability.

"Those who claim they are free from all worries are truly free from all worries if their improvement is very limited.

"Those whose practice deviates from Buddha's teaching can claim they are following the right way.

"Maitreya,

"I would not say that:

"Monks and nuns who love to talk can reach the state of oneness.

"Monks and nuns who love to engage in worldly affairs do not negatively affect their own cultivation.

"Those who practice purity will fall into the lower realms.

"Those who cultivate wisdom will engage in clamorous activities.

"Maitreya,

"I would not say that:

"Those who apply skillful means to help others are deviating from the right way.

"Those who do not seek benefits are lying.

"Those who refrain from making sacrifices for Dharma protection are right.

"Those who have overcome attachment will slander the right Dharma.

"Those who claim they are pure, while engaging in evil behavior, are pure."

Superior Bodhisattvas versus Inferior Bodhisattvas

Buddha told Maitreya Bodhisattva, "Maitreya, during the five hundred years of the Dharma declining period, there will be Bodhisattvas who are dull, lacking wisdom, dishonest, tricky and who deviate from the right path. Maitreya, you should help them."

Then Maitreya Bodhisattva asked, "World Honored One, during this declining period, in addition to the sixty confused Bodhisattvas, will there be other Bodhisattvas who are clouded by their sins?"

Buddha replied, "During this period, there will be many more Bodhisattvas who will be hampered by their sins. Some will gradually get rid of their sins by diligent practice. Others will continue to accumulate more sins."

Buddha continued, "Maitreya, during the five hundred years of the Dharma declining period there will be twenty superior Bodhisattvas born into this world with very few obstacles. They will be dignified, with power and authority, wise comportment, intelligence, wisdom, skills and compassion, as well as with scientific and mathematical skills. They won't show themselves. They will live simple lives and focus on cultivating virtues. In their myriad lifetimes they have renounced everything for the Bodhi path and accumulated countless merits. They risked their lives to protect the right Dharma; they lived quietly and practiced Dharma diligently, they did not look for benefits or offerings. They gained a thorough understanding of the essence of all Dharmas and gained eloquence. With Buddha's blessing they were able to expound the Dharma clearly and convincingly to all people. They gained great wisdom and were able to know the capacity of the people whom they helped. These twenty superior Bodhisattvas also openly pay tribute to their masters. They state clearly that they personally learned all the Dharmas directly from their masters."

Buddha said, "Maitreya, during the five hundred years of the Dharma declining period, there will be people, monks, nuns or laymen, who will not have wisdom or skill in means. They will be jealous of those achieved Bodhisattvas who expound the right Dharmas. They will ridicule and slander these Bodhisattvas and claim that what they say is not from Buddha but created by themselves. People should not believe them. Maitreya, as a result of their slander, the faith of the followers will be destroyed and they will desert the Bodhisattvas. Those vicious people say to each other that the achieved Bodhisattvas spread doctrines that do not comply with the Sutras and the precepts expounded by the Buddha. They accuse these Bodhisattvas of playing games like actors. People must not believe them. These mali-

cious and stupid people, controlled by demons will create serious sins for themselves and will fall into the three lower realms."

Buddha said, "Maitreya, in light of this situation, those achieved Bodhisattvas should be very careful to protect the right Dharma without showing their own merits or virtues."

Eloquent Abilities

Buddha told Maitreya Bodhisattva, "Maitreya, you should know that there are four kinds of eloquence promoted by all Buddhas. Also there are four kinds of eloquence prohibited by all Buddhas."

"What are the four kinds of eloquence promoted by all Buddhas?"

The Four Good Eloquent Abilities

"Those corresponding with benefits that help to liberate beings, not those with no benefits to beings.

"Those corresponding to the right Dharmas, not those against the right Dharmas.

"Those corresponding to eliminate delusions and worries, etc., not those that increase delusions and worries.

"Those corresponding to ultimate nirvana, and not to the cycle of birth and death."

"Bhiksus and laymen who wish to promote the Dharma should comply with the four principles of good eloquence. The listeners should follow and treat their teacher as Buddha, and accept it, because what they represent is the word of Buddha."

"If people slander and disrespect these four good eloquent abilities, and claim they are not from Buddha, it amounts to destroying the Dharma. As such they will fall into the three lower realms. Those who have committed these sins and wish to attain liberation should

repent and correct themselves. Also, people should not reject the right Dharma just because they dislike the person who expounds it."

The Four Bad Eloquent Abilities

Buddha said, "Maitreya, what are the four kinds of eloquence prohibited by all Buddhas?

"Those corresponding with non benefits, and not responding to benefits.

"Those corresponding with non-Dharma, and not corresponding to the real Dharma.

"Those corresponding with delusions and worries, and not corresponding to the elimination of delusions and worries.

"Those corresponding to the cycle of birth and death, and not corresponding to the merit of Nirvana." (Ultimate Liberation.)

"Maitreya, these four eloquent abilities are prohibited by all Buddhas."

At that time Maitreya Bodhisattva said, "World Honored One, if the eloquent ability increases the chance of being bonded by the cycle of birth and death, it will not be approved by all Tathagatas."

THE DIFFERENCES BETWEEN THE ACHIEVED AND BEGINNING BODHISATTVAS

Maitreya Bodhisattva asked Buddha about the difference between the achieved Bodhisattvas and the lowly ones.

Maitreya Bodhisattva asked, "World Honored One, as I understand the meaning of what you said in the five hundred years of the Dharma declining period, for Bodhisattvas who wish to eliminate their negative karmas, they must believe and fully understand the proper

conduct of Bodhisattvas. First they must not look for other's faults, and determine to work for the merits and virtues of the Tathagata (Buddha)."

Buddha answered, "That is right. That is right, Maitreya. Hence they must believe and fully understand the proper conduct of Bodhisattvas."

Buddha continued, "Maitreya, to benefit people, some achieved Bodhisattvas utilize convenient means which appear to contradict the principle of a Bodhisattva's conduct which is difficult for ordinary people to understand and believe. For example, a Srota-apanna (Buddhist stream-enterer) may purposely manifest the conduct of the worldly people in order to help people. In reality, he is different from worldly people in that worldly people are bound by their delusions of greed, anger, ignorance, etc. They may fall into the lower realms. The Srota-apannas are free from delusions and will not fall into the lower realms.

It is the same with the achieved Bodhisattvas. Although their habits have not been completely erased, they still are different from the beginning Bodhisattvas because their hearts are no longer clouded by any delusions. The Bodhisattvas with dull capacity are like the worldly stupid people full of delusions and lack of skills, and therefore cannot attain liberation. The achieved Bodhisattvas are armed with insightful wisdom and can destroy all their sins. As such, they will not fall into the three lower realms. They use the fire of their insightful wisdom to burn away all delusions. The power of wisdom and skillful means applied by the achieved Bodhisattvas are difficult for worldly people to comprehend."

WISDOM AND CULTIVATION

Then Maitreya Bodhisattva asked Buddha, "World Honored One, the beginning Bodhisattvas, who have left home, wish to acquire wisdom. What should they renounce and what should they practice?"

Buddha told Maitreya Bodhisattva, "Maitreya, if the beginning Bodhisattvas wish to acquire wisdom, they should know the faults of seeking worldly benefits and stay away from them. In addition, they should abandon clamorous activities of the marketplace, worldly and derisive speech, oversleeping and engaging in worldly business. Therefore, they should forgo seeking worldly benefits, and practice desirelessness, stay away from bustling activities, cultivate quietude, avoid worldly and derisive speech, stop oversleeping, observe the reality, improve themselves wherever and whenever, focus on cultivating the way, avoid worldly affairs, and be compassionate to all beings."

Buddha continued, "Maitreya, beginning Bodhisattvas who have left home wish to acquire wisdom. If they can't relinquish seeking worldly benefits and do not practice desirelessness, it will be impossible for them to gain wisdom.

FAULTS CATEGORY

Eleven Serious Obstacles

"Furthermore, if they can't give up bustling activities and can't live in a quiet place to practice Dharmas, it will also be impossible for them to gain wisdom.

"Not giving up bustling activities.

"Not staying in a quiet place.

"Engaging in worldly speech.

"Not learning and contemplating the real meaning of the Dharma.

"Oversleeping.

"Being sluggish and not awake.

"Not giving up worldly business.

"Worrying too much.

"Engaging in indecent and profane speech.

"Not practicing for liberation.

"Lacking compassion to all beings.

"Due to these obstacles, there is no possibility for the Bodhisattvas to acquire wisdom.

"Maitreya, therefore, Bodhisattvas who wish to acquire wisdom should renounce wrong things and practice the right Dharma. Why? Because wisdom comes from causes and conditions. Wisdom can't arise without causes and conditions. Wisdom is born when causes and conditions merge."

The Faults of Seeking Worldly Benefits by Bodhisattvas

At that time Maitreya Bodhisattva asked Buddha, "World Honored One, what are the faults of seeking worldly benefits by the Bodhisattvas? If Bodhisattvas can observe and understand the faults of seeking worldly benefits they will gladly give up those desires without worries."

Buddha said, "Maitreya,

"For the beginning Bodhisattvas, they should know that seeking worldly benefits breeds greed.

"They also should observe that seeking worldly benefits can destroy right thoughts and cause anger, due to jealousy and greed.

"Seeking worldly benefits can lead to stupidity and ignorance, because they will worry about gaining or losing them.

"Benefits can cause arrogance due to discrimination and jealousy.

"Worry about the intention of benefit donors causes anxiety.

"Greed distorts the heart and mind.

"Bodhisattvas will lose sight of the right path without shame.

"Benefits can cause egotism and arrogance which is prohibited by the Buddhas.

"Searching for benefits disrespects the right Dharma. Hence, Bodhisattvas lose the opportunity to attain liberation. Seeking worldly benefits and indulging in worldly pleasures they will fall into the fold of the devils.

"Seeking worldly benefits is the source of all evil deeds which will destroy all good roots.

"Greed breeds more greed like a hailstorm of greed.

"Currying favors without dignity from donors causes anxiety.

"Seeking benefits creates worries about losing benefits and material possessions.

"Seeking worldly benefits creates the loss of the four right efforts:

"The inability to put an end to existing evil.

"The inability to prevent evil rising.

"The inability to bring good into existence.

"The inability to develop existing good. As a result, the right Dharma disappears.

"Seeking worldly benefits creates the loss of the four contemplations:

"The body as impure and utterly filthy.

"Sensation as always resulting in suffering.

"Mind as impermanent, merely one sensation after another.

"Things in general as being dependent and without a nature of their own.

"Seeking worldly benefits causes Bodhisattvas to falsify attainment and feign miracles, which is against Buddha's teaching.

"Seeking worldly benefits causes Bodhisattvas to fight for benefits and creates hatred.

"Seeking worldly benefits causes Bodhisattvas to harbor bad thoughts and slander each other.

"Seeking worldly benefits causes Bodhisattvas to engage in worldly business with a calculating mind. Hence, they will lose peace and joy.

"Bodhisattvas seeking worldly benefits leads to regression in the Path. As such, they cannot attain stability, Samadhi and liberation.

"Bodhisattvas that lose wisdom resulting from greed will fall into hell, or into the realms of hungry ghosts or animals.

"Bodhisattvas will end up like Devadatta, in the lowest hell."

The Advantages of Not Seeking Worldly Benefits by Bodhisattvas

Buddha said,"Maitreya, beginning Bodhisattvas who observe and understand the faults of seeking worldly benefits and control their desires, will not generate worries. Why? Maitreya,

"Beginning Bodhisattvas will live a simple life and will avoid the above-mentioned faults.

"They will become pure Dharma vessels.

"Staying away from worldly benefits, left home or not they will be able to devote themselves to the Bodhi Path.

"They will joyfully live in the state of honesty, purity, equality and compassion that will lead to extraordinary bliss.

"They will live in peace without fear.

"Knowing the serious consequence of falling into the three lower realms, they will stay away from the wrong path.

"They will be free from obstruction without greed.

"They will attain liberation even in a bad environment.

"They will be blessed and praised by all Buddhas.

"They will be admired and protected by heavenly beings.

"They will stay in the Middle Way without attachment and dwell in Samadhi.

"They will maintain a straight mind and heart, without dishonesty. Even in the environment full of worldly desires they will be able to practice diligently without negligence.

"They will practice according to the true teaching.

"They will be respected by fellow cultivators."

Buddha said, "Maitreya, if there are wise Bodhisattvas who know the merits of giving up worldly benefits, they will happily live a simple life."

The Misdeeds of Indulging in the Activities of the Marketplace

At that time Maitreya Bodhisattva asked, "World Honored One, what are the misdeeds for Bodhisattvas who indulge in activities of the marketplace? If they truly understand the misdeeds of those activities they will be able to live in a quiet place without any troubles."

Buddha answered, "Maitreya, there are twenty misdeeds when beginning Bodhisattvas indulge in clamorous marketplace activities. They should observe closely and understand the misdeeds of those activities. Then they will be able to cultivate Dharma in a quiet place with solitude."

The Twenty Misdeeds

"Maitreya, what are the twenty misdeeds of indulging in clamorous activities?

"Bodhisattvas cannot protect the body.

"They cannot protect their speech.

"They cannot protect their hearts and minds.

"They foster greed.

"Indulging in clamorous activities leads to ignorance and stupidity.

"Bodhisattvas will indulge in worldly speech.

"They will forget the true teaching.

"They will respect and practice the wrong things.

"They will abandon the right Dharma.

"They will fall into the hands of devils.

"They no longer will be respectful and careful in life.

"They will become careless and sloppy, and will often make mistakes.

"Their thoughts will become scattered.

"They will no longer be able to learn the truth with diligence.

"They can't attain stillness.

"They will lack wisdom.

"They will take short cuts and achieve nothing.

"They will no longer respect Buddha.

"They will no longer respect the Dharma.

"They will no longer respect the Sangha."

Buddha told Maitreya Bodhisattva, "Maitreya, these are the twenty misdeeds of Bodhisattvas engaging in the clamorous activities of the marketplace."

Verses

At that time, Buddha restated the problems of engaging in activities of the marketplace with the following verses:

One must get rid of the five poisons: greed, anger, ignorance, ego and doubt.

One must stay away from market place activities.

If the mind is occupied by thoughts of clamorous activities, it is wrong.

Arrogance and distracting thoughts

Those who do not follow the precepts and love clamorous activities undermine the proper cultivation.

Stupid people love worldly views and theories.

They forget the truth.

They are lax and they have collective wandering thoughts, which should be avoided.

The Bhiksus (monks) who love the marketplace lose Buddha's teaching.

Their words no longer comply with reality, and hinder their meditation.

Those whose minds are constantly occupied with worldly affairs and indulge in scattered thoughts cannot attain stillness.

Their hearts and minds are always sluggish and dissipated.

They can never reach the right thoughts.

Those who take short cuts looking for instant success never go anywhere.

Indulging in market place activities makes one lose one's dignity and forbearance.

It shows that they do not love The Three Treasures: Buddha (Enlightenment), The Dharma (Truth), and The Sangha (Purity).

They give up desirelessness practice and indulge in worldly talk and speech.

In my past lives I gave up my body.

I gave up my eyes and my head in order to acquire the Dharma.

In my effort to seek The Supreme Way I never tired of learning the Dharma.

Those who learn little and feel complete are not really serious.

In one of my past lives I was a king.

I was anxious to learn four stanzas of the Dharma.

I renounced my Kingship, my family and wealth.

No one with wisdom is not anxiously learning the Dharma, and practicing diligently.

I have renounced everything, including divisive (mean and inappropriate) worldly speech.

Because for thousands of eons it is difficult to attain liberation.

People should be happy and determine to learn the wonderful Dharma.

If you want to attain liberation, which is the supreme merit, then you should not concern yourself with worldly affairs or make too much effort seeking a good life that will not bring you any great benefits.

There will be no victory.

Seeking worldly benefits will not help you reach Nirvana.

You should praise and practice the extraordinary Dharma.

All Bodhisattvas: Get together.

Discuss the essence of the Dharma only.

Do not engage in worldly speech.

It is difficult to acquire a human body.

Take every opportunity to learn the right Dharma.

Study the teaching of Buddha and cultivate meditation accordingly.

That is the right way.

In the future, after Buddha has entered Nirvana, the teaching of Buddha will gradually deteriorate.

Bhiksus will relapse.

They will not practice in quietude. Instead, they will enjoy worldly people and activities.

In order to seek worldly benefits they indulge in worldly activities.

They will indulge in worldly speech day and night.

Stupid people live in a dream and drift in great fear.

They realize they have violated The Precepts and will be born into The Three Lower Realms.

With a joyous heart and mind stay in solitary quietude.

If you dwell in a quiet place, cultivate The Supreme Path.

Do not look at the faults of other people and claim self-aggrandizement.

Arrogance is the root of laziness.

Don't look down upon "inferior persons" or any living being.

They may be following Buddha's teaching and may gradually attain liberation before you.

For Bhiksus (monks) who have broken The Precepts, there is still hope as long as they still have deep faith in The Three Treasures: The Buddha, The Dharma, and The Sangha, which is the cause of attaining liberation.

Therefore do not just look for the faults of other people.

The Three Poisons are hard to destroy.

Laziness is also difficult to overcome.

Laziness is normal in the human world.

Therefore, do not be surprised if a Bhiksu (monk) practices purity but still looks at the faults of other people.

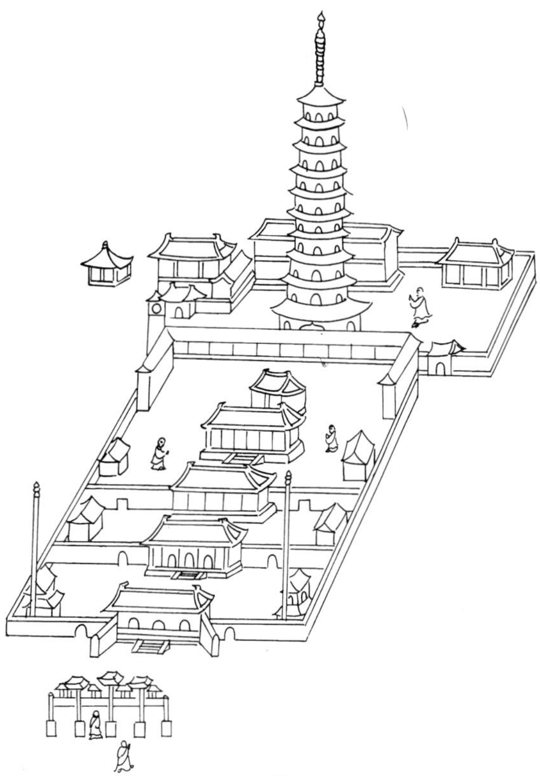

He is not really pure.

He is not practicing the real Dharma.

Individuals practicing the real Dharma according to Buddha's teaching should observe themselves constantly.

For those Bhiksus (monks) seeking The Path, they should remove all inappropriate speech and live joyously in a quiet environment, cultivating in solitude.

At that time Maitreya Bodhisattva said to Buddha, "World Honored One, people indulging in market place activities have so many faults, such as the loss of merits that brings no benefits, the increase of worries, the deviation from the right path and even the reality of falling into The Three Lower Realms. Bodhisattvas who are seeking the right Dharma, knowing the faults of indulging in market place activities will happily and quietly cultivate the Dharma in joyful solitude."

Worldly Speech

At that time, Maitreya Bodhisattva asked, "World Honored One, what are the faults of engaging in worldly speech? If the beginning Bodhisattvas can observe and fully understand the faults of engaging in worldly speech, they will be able to abide by the truth without worries."

Buddha replied, "Maitreya, the beginning Bodhisattvas should know that there are twenty faults of engaging in worldly speech. If they carefully observe and fully understand the faults of engaging in worldly speech and the merits of staying away from them, they will be able to abide by the truth without any worries."

Buddha continued, "Maitreya, these are the twenty faults:

Twenty Misdeeds

"Worldly speech gives rise to arrogance because the speaker focuses too much on worldly affairs. He knows too much about them and tends to disrespect those who are knowledgeable in the True Dharma.

"Worldly speech causes many arguments, disputes, conflicts, prejudice and preconceptions.

"Worldly speech makes one lose right thoughts and the ability to think in terms of the truth.

"Beginning Bodhisattvas who love worldly speech tend to do wrong things and engage in activities that will lead them into the three lower realms.

"Worldly speech is conductive to discrimination and the loss of the sense of equality. It also gives rise to intolerance.

"The minds of worldly speakers are hard and inflexible. Therefore, their meditation is obstructed and they cannot gain wisdom.

"Worldly speakers often talk in the wrong places and at the wrong times, causing troubles.

"Worldly speakers indulging in worldly speech cannot attain any level of liberation.

"Worldly speakers are despised by their protectors.

"Good people will stay away from them.

"Worldly speakers will be scolded by those who have attained liberation.

"Worldly speakers cannot settle with the real faith, and are wavering, unstable and full of regrets.

"Worldly speakers are enshrouded in dubiousness and oscillations.

"They act like actors who have lost their true selves.

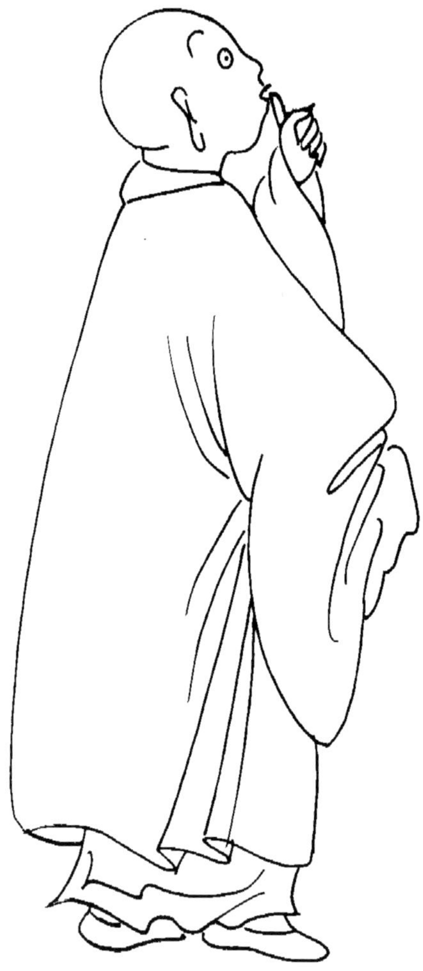

"Worldly speakers are defiled by worldly desires. They are swayed by the environment and can't control their lives.

"They can't see the truth. They even slander the Dharma.

"Whatever they seek and wish for is rarely fulfilled.

"Their minds can't maintain balance. They are deserted by other people.

"They are confused and unable to see the right path. They associate with negative friends.

"All the senses of worldly speakers are clouded by worries.

"Maitreya, these are the twenty faults for Bodhisattvas engaging in worldly speech."

Verses

At that time, the Buddha restated the faults of indulging in worldly speech in the following verses:

Arrogant people disrespect real knowledge.

Their inflexibility causes disputes.

They forget the right teaching.

These are the faults of indulging in worldly speech.

Worldly speech keeps one away from the right thoughts.

One cannot attain and remain in stillness and peace.

One loses patience in the cultivation of the Dharma.

With too much delusion therefore, one can't regulate the heart peacefully.

One can't attain Samadhi (through putting things down).

Nor can one achieve tranquility (through penetrating the reality of things).

These are the faults of indulging in worldly speech.

One disrespects the Dharma teacher.

Those who love worldly speech and views have no real wisdom.

These are the faults of indulging in worldly speech.

One is disrespected by heavenly beings, and also despised by the protectors.

One loses the ability of eloquence.

These are the faults of indulging in worldly speech.

One is scolded by people who have attained The Way.

People indulging in worldly speech waste their lives.

These are the faults of indulging in worldly speech.

Those indulging in worldly speech are defective in the cultivation of The Path.

Therefore, they deviate from the Supreme Path.

They will fall into the lower realms after death.

These are the faults of indulging in worldly speech.

The mind and the heart waver because of doubts.

They are just like the wind blowing through the grass, because they lack real wisdom.

These are the faults of indulging in worldly speech.

They are just like an actor on a stage, loving words of empty praise which are meaningless.

People who love worldly speech are just like actors.

These are the faults of indulging in worldly speech.

Indulging in worldly speech leads to worldly desires and impels one to follow a deviant path.

These are the faults of indulging in worldly speech.

Wishes cannot be fulfilled.

When the heart and mind is crooked and full of arguments one has lost the right path.

These are the faults of indulging in worldly speech.

Stupid people are contented with petty benefits.

Their hearts and minds are always in a wavering state, like monkeys who never can remain still.

These are the faults of indulging in worldly speech.

One loses real wisdom.

The heart and mind are not awake.

One is controlled and manipulated by bad people.

These are the faults of indulging in worldly speech.

One is confused by the Six Senses: sight, hearing, smell, taste, touch and mind as well as the faculty of thought.

One is always embroiled with worries and delusions.

These are the faults of indulging in worldly speech.

Stupid people love worldly speech.

They waste their lives.

They are better off focusing on the meaning of one thing for then they will be benefitted without limit.

Like the sweet taste of sugar in the sugar cane, although the sweetness flows through the skin and the joints of the cane, it does not come from them, yet we get the taste of sweetness.

The skin and the joints are like worldly speech.

The sweet taste is the real meaning.

Therefore, we should give up empty worldly speech and focus on real meaning.

The wise Bodhisattvas know the faults of worldly speech.

They always ponder over the merits and virtues of the Supreme reality, the flavor and essence of the Dharma as well as the wonderful fragrance of liberation.

The wise people will be joyful.

People should give up useless worldly speech and always enjoy contemplating the meaning of the Supreme Reality.

This is the supreme Dharma, which is always praised by all Buddhas.

Therefore, people of wisdom always joyfully practice diligently.

At that time Maitreya Bodhisattva said to Buddha, "World Honored One, it is wonderful that you have spoken so beautifully on the faults of indulging in worldly speech, and have explained the benefits and merits as well as the real meaning of the right way of practice. Bodhisattvas who are sincerely seeking the essential wisdom will not love empty worldly speech."

The Twenty Faults of Oversleeping

Maitreya Bodhisattva asked, "World Honored One, what are the faults of oversleeping? Bodhisattvas should observe and practice the Dharma diligently without worries."

Twenty Faults

Buddha answered, "Maitreya, there are twenty faults of oversleeping for beginning Bodhisattvas. If they can observe carefully and understand the faults of oversleeping, They will be inspired to practice diligently and joyfully without feeling tired. Maitreya, what are The twenty Faults of Oversleeping?

"Laziness and lethargy.

"One physically becoming heavier, and thus obese.

"One's color sallows.

"The chance of sickness and disease increase.

"The body temperature becomes low and weak.

"One develops poor digestion.

"One develops bed sores.

"One is unable to practice the Dharma diligently.

"One becomes dull and stupid.

"One becomes weak in wisdom.

"One's skin grows pale and pallid.

"One is no longer respected by heavenly protectors.

"One's movement is slow and unintelligent.

"One is full of worries.

"The seed of bad habits cloud the heart and mind.

"One lacks energy and loses interest in the good Dharma.

"One's good deeds decrease, and one's bad deeds increase.

"One's behavior is negative and bad.

"One dislikes diligence.

"Therefore, one is looked down upon by others.

"Maitreya, these are the twenty faults of oversleeping."

Verses

At that time, Buddha restated the faults of oversleeping in the following verses:

One's body is heavy and without deportment.

One is lax, idle, inactive and cannot take responsibility.

One has no color.

These are the faults of oversleeping.

One is often sick and full of worries.

One has poor health.

The four major elements of earth, air, water and fire are unbalanced.

One has poor digestion.

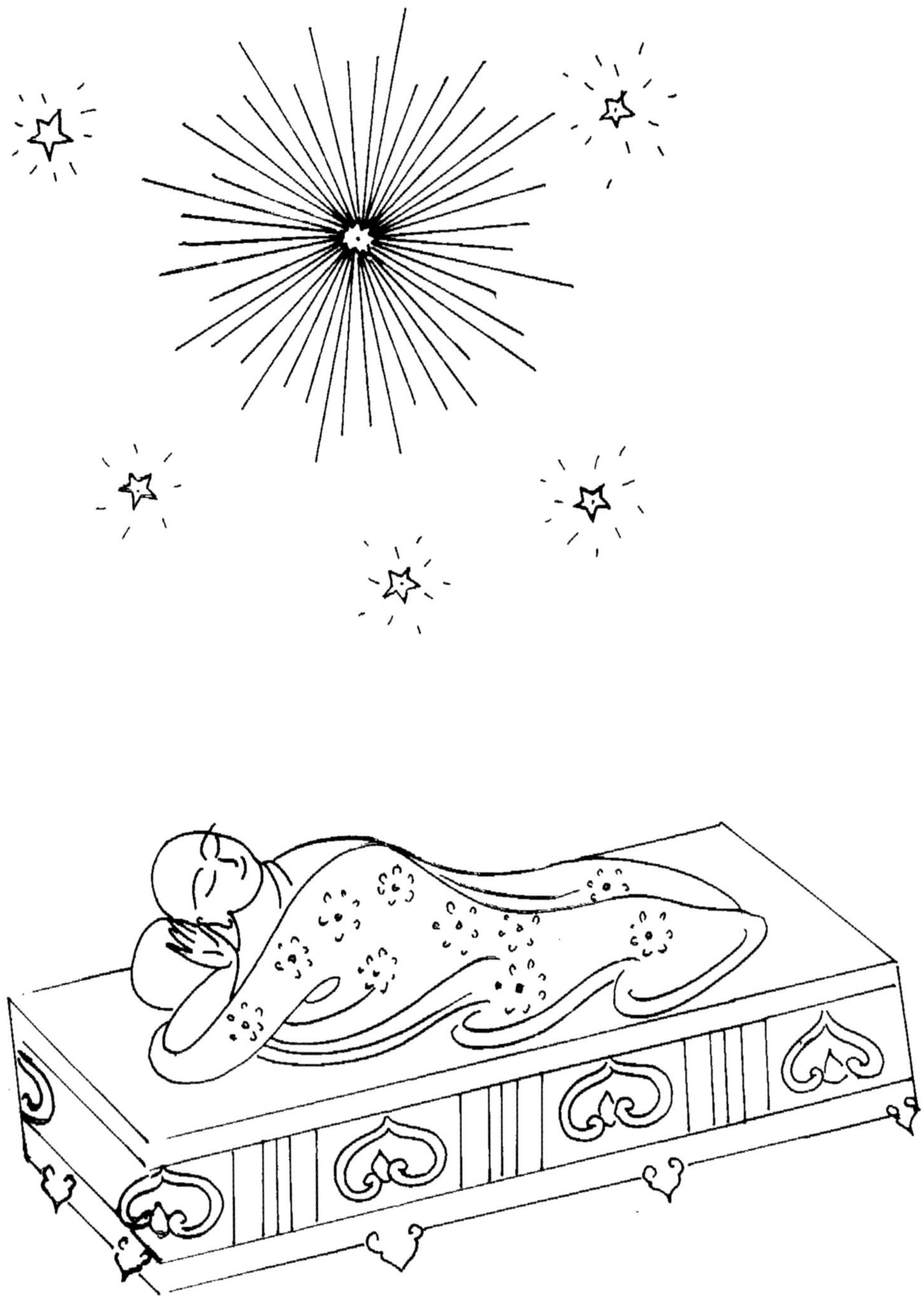

One is without luster.

One's voice is hoarse and unclear.

These are the faults of oversleeping.

One develops bedsores due to sleeping day and night.

One has parasites inside the body.

These are the faults of oversleeping.

One no longer practices diligently, nor can one produce wealth.

One has lots of dreams but there is no awakening.

These are the faults of oversleeping.

Because one is lax, one becomes stupid and perplexed.

One is full of scattered thoughts and opinions.

It is difficult for one to change.

One's intelligence decreases.

One's stupidity and ignorance increases.

One is low in spirit and lacks determination.

These are the faults of oversleeping.

Even living in a quiet place, one is always idle.

Therefore evil enters.

These are the faults of oversleeping.

One is muddle-headed and loses right thoughts.

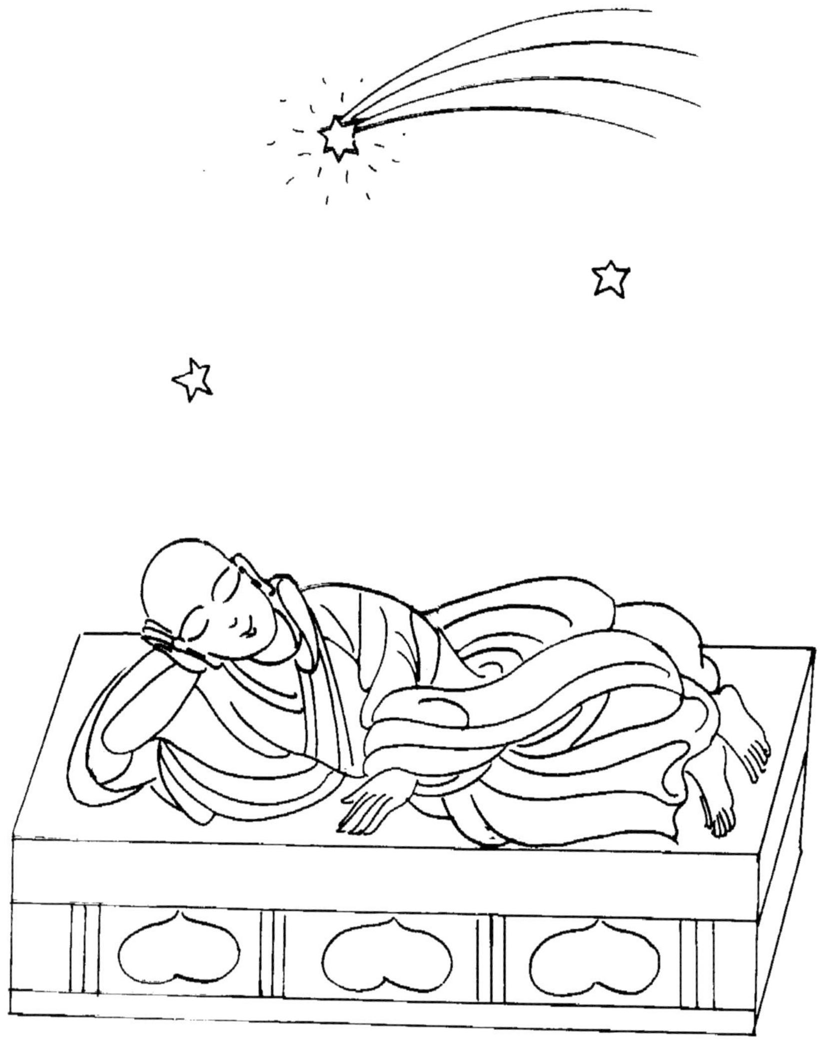

One becomes forgetful and does not understand the sutras.

When hearing the Dharma, one often misunderstands and forgets their real meanings.

These are the faults of oversleeping.

Ignorance and stupidity lead to confusion.

One lives with constant worries and delusions.

One's heart is not at peace.

These are the faults of oversleeping.

One's merits and virtues are reduced and damaged.

One is full of anxiety and feels remorse and regret.

One's worries increase.

These are the faults of oversleeping.

Good people will stay away from him.

One no longer makes the effort to seek the right Dharma.

Instead, one is engaged in wrong things.

These are the faults of oversleeping.

One is unable to obtain joy from practicing the Dharma.

Merits and virtues are damaged and decreased.

One stays away from the right Dharma.

These are the faults of oversleeping.

One's heart is weak.

One lacks joy.

The limbs are weak and one is physically feeble.

These are the faults of oversleeping.

Even though one is aware of his own lazy idleness, he is still jealous of diligent practitioners, and loves to bad mouth them.

These are the faults of oversleeping.

The wise people know the faults of oversleeping.

They stay away from oversleeping.

Stupid people only increase wrong thoughts.

Therefore they damage their own merits and virtues without any benefits.

The wise people always practice diligently.

They always cultivate the pure path diligently.

Therefore, they enjoy happiness and peace.

As such, they are praised by all Buddhas.

All the skills in this world and other worlds can only be achieved by diligent efforts and devotion.

Wise people should learn these skills.

If people are interested in pursuing the Bodhi Path, they should know the faults of oversleeping and devote great effort for it and keep awake and be ashamed of oversleeping.

That is why wise people always cultivate diligently and stay away from oversleeping and protect as well as nourish the Bodhi seed.

At that time, Maitreya Bodhisattva said to Buddha, "World Honored One, since the love of oversleeping has so many faults, if people hear them and still do not concern themselves about them, and continue to indulge in oversleeping, and do not start to practice diligently, then we know that these people are very stupid. If Bodhisattvas desire to seek Supreme Enlightenment, but after hearing the above remarks, and understanding the merits and benefits of practicing the right Dharmas, are still lax and do not practice diligently—then they are very wrong."

The Faults of Bodhisattvas Doing Worldly Business

At that time Maitreya Bodhisattva asked, "World Honored One, what are the problems of Bodhisattvas doing worldly business? When they observe and recognize the faults of doing worldly business they will stop doing it and practice the Bodhi Path diligently."

Buddha said, "Maitreya, the beginning Bodhisattvas should know that there are twenty kinds of faults in doing worldly business. If they observe and fully understand those faults, they will stay away from them and devote themselves to cultivating the Bodhi Path diligently."

Twenty Faults

"Maitreya, what are the twenty faults of bodhisattvas doing worldly business?

> "Beginning Bodhisattvas indulging in worldly business arouse the five poisons, thus leading to inferior activities.
>
> "Beginning Bodhisattvas who engage in worldly business will be looked down upon by Bhiksus who practice the Dharma.
>
> "They will also be looked down upon and scolded by Bhiksus who have attained stillness.
>
> "They will always worry about the success or failure of their business. They can't get out of the birth and death cycle.

"Bodhisattvas who receive offerings from laymen but those who do not practice vigorously for enlightenment will be born into the animal realms.

"Whenever worldly Bodhisattvas see valuable things, their desire arises to possess them.

"They will always try to do more business and expand their existing business.

"Their minds are always occupied by their businesses, and are totally consumed with losing and gaining.

"Worldly Bodhisattvas develop the attitude of arrogance and obnoxiousness because of the wealth and fame they have gained from business.

"Their minds are consumed by their worldly business and they are no longer on the Path.

"Worldly Bodhisattvas develop the taste of worldly pleasures and material enjoyments. This gives rise to more greed.

"They avoid places where there is little chance for them to acquire worldly benefits, offerings and fame.

"Worries create obstacles for those on the Path.

"Worldly Bodhisattvas love to associate with laymen in order to secure worldly fame and benefits.

"Worldly Bodhisattvas worry about their worldly business. Hence their Dharma practice becomes a façade.

"All conversation is focused on their worldly business.

"All their speech is worldly.

"Because they know how to do worldly business they become arrogant.

"They only look at other people's faults and do not reflect upon themselves.

"They even despise those who are able to expound the Dharma.

"Maitreya, these are the twenty Kinds of Faults of Bodhisattvas Indulging in Worldly Business."

Verses

At that time, Buddha wished to restate the faults of engaging in worldly business in the following verses:

Bodhisattvas who absorb themselves in worldly business are far away from the Bodhi Path.

They miss the great benefits of attaining liberation.

Those who follow Buddha's teaching and those who devote themselves to practice with great vigor will scold those who indulge in worldly business.

These are the faults of engaging in worldly business:

Those who pursue worldly business can never be free from the cycle of birth and death.

In reality they have given up the cause of liberation.

Yet they continue to receive offerings without a cause.

These are the faults of engaging in worldly business.

Those who engage in worldly business love to receive money and valuables.

They become worried and unhappy if they do not get them, and conduct themselves in inferior behavior.

These are the faults of engaging in worldly business.

Inwardly they are full of worries, desires, anger, jealousies, arrogance, etc.

Outwardly they succumb to varieties of temptations.

They are just like caged birds.

These are the faults of engaging in worldly business.

Those who engage in worldly business always worry and lament about their business and are always in a nervous, uneasy and tormented state.

Other people do not believe their words.

These are the faults of engaging in worldly business.

They cannot accept teaching from those who have attained.

They disregard rules and violate the Precepts.

These are the faults of engaging in worldly business.

Those who engage in worldly business have minds that are full of wandering thoughts.

They busily work on worldly business.

But they can't cultivate stillness and wisdom.

These are the faults of engaging in worldly business.

Those who engage in worldly business constantly grow in desires.

They love and indulge in worldly pleasures.

They never feel satisfaction, contentment or that they ever have enough.

They are only happy when there are benefits.

They worry and are miserable when there are no benefits.

They are full of desires, are stingy, and are without compassion.

These are the faults of engaging in worldly business.

Those who engage in worldly business lack compassion. They only look for self benefits without any concern for the condition of others.

Their negative activities continue to grow.

They are overcome by desires.

These are the faults of engaging in worldly business.

Good teachers depart from them.

Bad people come close to them.

They exclude those that follow the Precepts.

These are the faults of engaging in worldly business.

Day and night there are no other thoughts except for worldly benefits.

They have no interest in cultivating merits and virtues.

These are the faults of engaging in worldly business.

Those who engage in worldly business always look for worldly cleverness.

They have no interest in words that will help them in liberation.

Instead, they indulge in frivolous talk.

These are the faults of indulging in worldly business.

Those who engage in worldly business are proud to be knowledgeable in worldly affairs and activities.

They become arrogant and look down upon other Bhiksus (monks).

They are just like drunks.

These are the faults of engaging in worldly business.

Those who engage in worldly business always look at the faults of others.

They never see their own faults.

They look down upon and slander people of morality.

These are the faults of engaging in worldly business.

These are stupid people.

They have no good skill or means.

Yet, they look down upon those who promote the Dharma.

These are the faults of engaging in worldly business.

Bodhisattvas engaging in worldly business are inferior.

This inferior behavior produces all kinds of faults.

No wise people would practice such behavior.

The extraordinary pure practice possesses all merits and virtues.

That is why all wise people love to practice it.

Those Bodhisattvas who love to do worldly business will be scolded by wise people.

It amounts to giving up great benefits for little gain.

Wise people stay away from these inferior activities.

They look for and practice the superior Dharmas.

These wise people are always praised and blessed by all Buddhas.

At that time Maitreya Bodhisattva said to Buddha, "World Honored One, Bodhisattvas who give up superior practices and indulge in inferior activities are truly lacking in wisdom."

THE REAL LEFT-HOME BODHISATTVAS

At that time, Buddha told Maitreya Bodhisattva, "Maitreya, I tell you truthfully, if beginning Bodhisattvas do not cultivate and correct their behavior according to the teaching, do not eliminate their delusions, do not practice the Dharma, and do not study to gain knowledge of the teaching, I say that they are not the real left-home Bodhisattvas."

"Of those who have eliminated their delusions; true wisdom has arisen; true wisdom has been accomplished; they do not involve themselves in worldly business. I say that they are the real cultivators of Tathagata's teaching.

"If Bodhisattvas love to do worldly business which they should not do, I say that they are still entangled in the cycle of birth and death. Thus, beginning Bodhisattvas should not associate with them. If Bodhisattvas engage in many worldly affairs, even if they were to build a myriad number of treasure pagodas, enough to fill entire space, they would not make me happy. I would not consider that is their respect or offerings to me.

"Maitreya, but if Bodhisattvas who practice the Dharma for the supreme wisdom, receive, practice and expound even as few as four lines of verse for others, I will consider these are the true offerings to me. Why? Because all Buddhas come from broad and profound wisdom, not from doing worldly business.

"Maitreya, if those Bodhisattvas who are deeply involved in worldly affairs induce others to follow them in worldly business it will create more obstacles for them as a result. They will not be able to gain any non-worldly benefits. Why? Because all merits come from "wisdom", not from worldly business. Therefore, Bodhisattvas doing worldly business should not involve others and create obstacles for Bodhisattvas who study, practice the Dharma, and speak about them to others. They should not involve and create obstacles for those Bodhisattvas who study, practice the Dharma and speak for others as well as cultivate Samadhi.

"Maitreya, they should associate with, serve, respect, and make offerings to those Bodhisattvas who study, practice the Dharma, and speak for others. Also, they should associate with, serve, respect, and make offerings to those Bodhisattvas who study, practice the Dharma, and speak for others as well as cultivate Samadhi diligently.

"The Tathagata will happily approve such good activities if one serves, respects, and makes offerings to those Bodhisattvas who devote themselves diligently to cultivating "wisdom." One will gain unlimited merits. Why? Because the "wisdom" is the supreme element beyond all and can lead to ultimate liberation. Therefore, Maitreya, for those Bodhisattvas who truly want to practice the Bodhi Path, they should cultivate wisdom diligently."

DERISIVE SPEECH

At that time, Maitreya Bodhisattva said to Buddha, "World Honored One, that is very well said regarding the various faults of beginning Bodhisattvas indulging in the hustle and bustle of worldly affairs, worldly business, worldly speech and oversleeping. What are the faults of derisive speech? Through observation, so that Bodhisattvas will understand these faults and this will enable them to dwell in stillness without conflicts." Buddha said, "The faults of beginning Bodhisattvas engaging in derisive speech are countless. Here I only briefly point out the following twenty faults:

The Twenty Faults of Derisive Speech

"Derisive speech generates misery and distress in this lifetime.

"Derisive speech increases anger and causes people to lose their patience, tolerance and endurance.

"Derisive speech irritates people and causes ill-will and hatred in return.

"Therefore, the devil loves derisive speech, because the derisive speaker becomes part of the devil.

"The roots of virtue and goodness cannot grow.

"The existing roots of virtue and goodness regresses.

"Derisive speech leads to conflict and hatred.

"Derisive speech creates hell for the derisive speaker.

"Derisive speech results in ugly and bad karma.

"The tongue becomes sluggish and one cannot speak well.

"Any Dharma given to the derisive speaker will be unable to be remembered or acted upon.

"The derisive speaker will be unable to listen to or understand the Dharma, and hence will be unable to attain Enlightenment.

"Good people will leave the derisive speaker.

"The derisive speaker will attract bad people.

"Even though the derisive speaker practices the Dharma, he will not be able to attain it.

"Other people will speak unpleasantly about him.

"In life after life, the derisive speaker will be full of doubts because he will be covered by bad Karma.

"The derisive speaker will often be born in the wrong place, with no chance to hear the Dharma.

"Even though the derisive speaker wants to do good, he will face many obstacles.

"Even though the derisive speaker may have material and spiritual enjoyments, he will still have to encounter lots of jealousy and hatred.

"These are the twenty faults of Bodhisattvas who indulge in derisive speech."

Verses

At that time Buddha restated the faults of derisive speech with the following verses:

Derisive speech causes misery and distress in this life time.

It causes one to lose the ability to endure insults, disgrace and causes anger.

It causes the thought of harming others.

These are the faults of engaging in derisive speech.

Devils and their followers are very happy with derisive speakers.

Devils and their followers cause one to lose all good Dharmas.

These are the faults of engaging in derisive speech.

Goodness cannot emerge.

Often one will become embroiled in conflicts, disagreements, and arguments.

As a result, this creates evil deeds and ensures that one will be reborn into the lower realms.

These are the faults of engaging in derisive speech.

One will be born ugly into a lowly family.

One will have difficulty expressing oneself, and will stumble over words when speaking.

These are the faults of engaging in derisive speech.

One cannot practice the Dharma, and even though one hears the instructions, the Dharma is unable to enter the heart.

One often stays away from good people.

These are the faults of engaging in derisive speech.

Bad people will come close to derisive speakers.

As a result, it is difficult for derisive speakers to stay out of the lower realms.

One often hears unpleasant speech.

These are the faults of engaging in derisive speech.

Wherever one is, the derisive speaker will always have doubts and be in a state of confusion.

Hence, the derisive speaker cannot understand the Dharma.

These are the faults of derisive speech.

One will always be born into the eight conditions, in which it is difficult to see a Buddha or hear his Dharma, and far away from any place with Buddhism.

Derisive speech brings no benefits.

These are the faults of derisive speech.

Derisive speech brings all kinds of obstacles.

One loses correct thinking.

Often one is faced with hatred and jealousy.

These are the faults of derisive speech.

All these faults come from derisive speech.

Therefore, people with wisdom should swiftly avoid it.

Those who indulge in derisive speech have difficulty attaining the Ultimate Truth.

People with wisdom should not befriend those who indulge in derisive speech.

People with wisdom should also stay away from places of argument and disputes.

Because these places will only bring trouble.

People with wisdom should also stay away from those places as far as possible.

In addition, one should never build one's home near places of disputes.

Therefore, people who have renounced the world, like monks and nuns, should stay away from those places of arguments and disputes.

The renounced people, who own no property, who have no family, wife, or servants, have no fame or honored position.

There is no reason for them to get involved in arguments and disputes.

People who have renounced the world should live in a quiet, simple place, dress in a simple Dharma robe, and practice in quietude.

They will be respected by all the Divine Spirits.

People who have renounced the world should nurture the ability to endure insults, suffering and disgrace.

Those who indulge in derisive speech cause evil deeds and create a hateful heart.

They will be born into the lower realms.

Hence, people should cultivate fortitude.

The punishments and sufferings of inmates in jails all come from arguments, disputes and derisive speech.

Derisive speakers often meet bad people so they cannot make any progress, which does not help their reputation, and therefore they cannot bring any happiness to themselves.

If they give up arguments and disputes, then devils cannot find a way to them.

Without derisive speech, friends will not leave them, and they often will meet good people and find peace.

When one attains stillness and purity, then all negative karmas will disappear.

All devils will be subjugated.

It is important to nurture endurance in order to bear with insults, slander, and disgrace.

Arguments, disputes and conflicts have infinite numbers of faults.

Discarding them leads to good deeds.

All cultivators should cultivate endurance.

At that time Maitreya Bodhisattva said to Buddha, "World Honored One, your marvelous exposition on the faults of derisive speech should help all Bodhisattvas to wake up. World Honored One, during the first five hundred years of the declining period of Buddhism, can Bodhisattvas having heard your exposition on the faults of disputes and conflicts, repent and stay free from worries and troubles?"

Buddha told Maitreya Bodhisattva,

"Maitreya, during the first five hundred years of the declining period of Buddhism, there will be very few Bodhisattvas who can repent and be free from worries and conflicts. Instead, there will be many Bodhisattvas who are hard and stubborn. They will not respect each other and will be arrogant. They will bad mouth each other. Although they have heard the profound meaning of the exposition, and the remarkable merits that ensue from it, and they accept, study, practice and promote this sutra, yet because their negative karmas are too heavy, they will not be able to follow it properly. Therefore, they will not be able to attain the great merits. Hence, their doubts will arise, and they will no longer believe nor practice nor promote Buddha's teaching. They no longer promote the Dharma.

"At that time, The King of Evil saw the Bodhisattvas listening to my discourse on this Sutra. He pretended to be a monk and came to their abode. Derisively, he declared to the

Bodhisattvas that all Sutras were written by worldly writers and not by the True Buddha. Therefore, he said, Bodhisattvas will not be able to receive benefits and merits from this Sutra. Because the Bodhisattvas were deceived and misled by the Devil, doubts and confusion about the most profound sutras arose in their minds. Hence they no longer studied, practiced or promoted the profound sutras anymore."

Buddha continued, "Maitreya, those stupid people could not understand the sutra because of their negative karma. They could not attain to the extraordinary merits from practice.

"Know this: only when negative karma disappears can one reap such extraordinary merits."

THE TEN MAJOR VOWS OF THE HEART

At that time Maitreya Bodhisattva asked Buddha, "World Honored One, as you said, Amitabha Buddha's Western Paradise has infinite merits and benefits. If there are sentient beings who can bring about the Ten Major Vows of the Heart and concentrate single-mindedly evoking and reciting Amitabha's holy name, they will be reborn into His Pure Land when they leave this world."

Maitreya Bodhisattva continued, "World Honored One, what are the Ten Major Vows of the Heart that can cause those individuals to be reborn into the Western Pure Land?"

Buddha told Maitreya Bodhisattva, "Maitreya, The Ten Major Vows of the Heart can't come from those stupid, ignorant, evil, worried or deluded individuals. They are not capable of opening their hearts.

"The Ten Major Vows of the Heart are as follows:

> "We vow to evoke a great compassion for all sentient beings and give them happiness without any thought of harming them.
>
> "We vow to invoke our great compassion to alleviate all pain and misery from all sentient beings, without causing them worries, delusions or imposition.

"We joyfully vow to protect and adhere to all good and white (pure) Dharmas, even if it means sacrificing our lives to protect them.

"We vow to honor and respect all Dharmas taught by Buddha and to treat all Dharmas equally without discrimination.

"We vow not to seek worldly benefits, but to maintain a joyous pure heart and respect all.

"We vow to remember at all times the goal of attaining Buddhahood.

"We vow to respect all sentient beings without being arrogant or looking down upon anyone.

"We vow not to become attached to worldly knowledge and remain determined to attain Enlightenment.

"We vow to work on all good roots and maintain a pure heart without being tainted.

"We vow to detach from appearances of any forms and keep the heart pure and open."

Buddha continued, "Maitreya, these are the Ten Major Vows of the Heart. Those who practice them will surely be born in Amitabha's Western Paradise. Maitreya, if a person has one vow, he will have all. Each one includes the other nine, they are all mutually inclusive. He will be born into the Western Paradise."

III THE NAME OF THE SUTRA

At that time, Ananda said to Buddha, "World Honored One, your discourse reveals the real merits of the Tathagata, bringing about the extraordinary ways of cultivation of the Bodhi Path for Bodhisattvas.

"World Honored One, how do you name this Sutra? How do we receive and practice it?"

Buddha said, "The name of this sutra is:

> "THE REVELATION OF THE EXTRAORDINARY WAYS
> OF BODHI PATH CULTIVATION FOR BODHISATTVAS.

"It is also named:

> "MAITREYA BODHISATTVA'S INQUIRY SUTRA.

"You should believe, receive and practice it according to the meaning of the name of this Sutra."

After hearing what the Buddha had said, all those in the assembly rejoiced, believed, received and practiced accordingly.

Tze-si "Jesse" Huang is a professional writer and translator and native Chinese. He was born in Chungking, the youngest of ten children. After facing and overcoming the trials of both survival and becoming educated, recorded in his *Journey to the Unknown* (Fons Vitae, 2014), he eventually immigrated to the U.S.A. He attended New York University and Columbia University for post graduate studies. In 1975, he met his wife, the renown children's book author and illustrator, Demi. In the United States he worked as a financial analyst and manager in several companies while continuing to pursue his love of writing and translating from his native Chinese into English. His award winning title, *Master of Zen: Extraordinary Teachings from Hui Neng's Altar Sutra,* is an example of his excellent work. In 1990, both Tze-si Huang and his wife, Demi, represented the United States at the First Children's International Book Conference in Beijing.

Demi is an award-winning illustrator of numerous books for children, including biographies of spiritual figures such as Jesus, Muhammad, Buddha, the Dalai Lama, Saint Francis of Assisi, Lao Tzu, al-Ghazzali, and Joan of Arc. Her books include *The Empty Pot, The Nightingale, The Emperor's New Clothes*, and *Gandhi*, which was named the *New York Times* Best Illustrated Book and received the Oppenheim Toy Portfolio Platinum Award.